Introduction

Welcome to my Healthy Handbook to Cooking in Spain, the Dips & Salads Edition

I am a big fan of homemade dips and salads. They can be a healthy option for daily consumption as they are usually low in calories and high in nutrients.

Dips prepared with healthy ingredients can provide a boost of protein and healthy fats. Dips can also be combined with vegetables such as carrots, cucumbers or peppers, which add even more nutrients to your meal.

Salads are often packed with a variety of fresh vegetables and fruits that provide important vitamins, minerals and fibre. Eating a salad before a meal can also help you feel full and satisfied, which can prevent overeating.

Both dips and salads are often made from fresh, raw ingredients that require little or no cooking, which can save on energy costs.

Dips can be prepared in minutes and require little cooking. Simply purée or blend the ingredients and you are ready to go.

Salads are also quick and easy to prepare. Many salads are easy to prepare by chopping up fresh vegetables and tossing everything together with a simple dressing.

They can also be prepared in advance and stored in the fridge, making them a great option for meal preparation or for guests.

So friends, enjoy and feel free to drop me an email.
Big Love from Karla
info@Darocas.com

TABLE OF CONTENTS

Welcome to my Healthy Handbook to Cooking in Spain, the Dips & Salads Edition..1

Dips are a versatile and practical eating option, especially on holiday..3
PRICKLY PEANUT DIP...4
ROASTED ARTICHOKE HEARTS DIP..5
ROASTED CAULIFLOWER FLORETS DIP..6
ROASTED RED PEPPER DIP..7
OLD FAVOURITE ONION DIP..8
CREAMY COCONUT DIP..9
CREAMY CASHEW DIP..10
SUN-DRIED TOMATO N BEAN DIP..11
SIMPLE CHICKPEA DIP...12
SPICED BEAN DIP...13

Salads are the first choice for many people when it comes to eating healthy, even on holiday... 14
SOUTH SEAS SALAD..15
SOUTH SEAS CHICKPEA SALAD..16
RED BEAN N AVOCADO SALAD..17
WHITE BEAN N FRESH SALAD... 18
FRESH BURGOS LACTOSE-FREE CHEESE SALAD...................................... 19
SPANISH CAPRESE SALAD..20
FRESH SUMMER SALAD WITH SOYA BITES..21
PEANUT LOVERS SOYA SALAD..22
MEXICAN CORN SALAD..23
ROASTED RED PEPPER N PINE NUT SALAD..24
WALNUT N CRANBERRY SALAD..25
QUINOA SUMMER SALAD..26
ASIAN QUINOA SALAD...27
CHICKPEA N BABY SPINACH SALAD...28
CHICKEN N GREEN OLIVE SALAD...29
CHICKEN N ALMOND SALAD..30
MIXED GREENS N BLACK OLIVE SALAD...31
LENTIL FUSILLI PASTA SALAD...32
PARDINA LENTIL SALAD..33

TRANSLATED GLOSSARY INGREDIENTS & SPICES..34

Dips

Dips are a versatile and practical eating option, especially on holiday.

Whether you are entertaining guests, taking a snack for the beach or just looking for a quick and easy meal, dips are a delicious and nutritious solution.

Vegetables are the perfect accompaniment to dips, but sometimes you want something different. In Spain, we have fun dipping sticks called Picos. These are little bread sticks that are available at Mercadona in wholemeal and gluten-free.

Mercadona also has delicious, firm corn crisps, which are also great for dipping.

Whole Wheat Picos

Great Dipper!

3.

PRICKLY PEANUT DIP

Ingredients:
- 1/2 cup peanut powder
- 1/2 cup plain Greek yogurt
- 1 tablespoon honey
- 1/2 teaspoon salt
- 1/2 teaspoon garlic powder
- 1/2 teaspoon onion powder
- 1/4 teaspoon cumin
- 1/4 teaspoon sweet and / or hot paprika
- Fresh parsley or coriander, chopped (optional)

Directions:
1. In a medium bowl, combine the peanut powder, Greek yogurt, honey, salt, garlic powder, onion powder, cumin, and paprika. Stir well to combine.
2. If the mixture seems too thick, you can add a tablespoon or two of water to thin it out.
3. Taste the dip and adjust the seasoning to your liking. If you want it spicier, you can add a pinch of cayenne pepper.
4. Cover the dip and refrigerate for at least 30 minutes before serving. This will allow the flavours to meld together.
5. When ready to serve, sprinkle chopped parsley or coriander on top of the dip for a pop of freshness and colour.
6. Serve with your favourite vegetables, crackers, or Pico sticks for dipping. Enjoy!

ROASTED ARTICHOKE HEARTS DIP

Ingredients:
- 1 cup artichokes hearts, chopped
- 1/4 cup mayonnaise
- 1/4 cup Greek Yogurt
- 1/4 cup grated Parmesan cheese
- 2 cloves garlic, minced
- 1 tablespoon lemon juice
- Salt and pepper, to taste
- Olive oil

Instructions:
1. Preheat your oven to 375 °F (190 °C).
2. In a small bowl, toss the chopped baby artichokes with olive oil and a pinch of salt and pepper. Place them on a baking sheet and roast for about 20–25 minutes, or until tender and lightly browned. Remove from the oven and let cool.
3. In a medium bowl, mix together the mayonnaise, Greek Yogurt, grated Parmesan cheese, minced garlic, and lemon juice. Stir until well combined.
4. Add the roasted baby artichokes to the bowl with the dip mixture and stir until everything is evenly distributed.
5. Taste the dip and adjust seasoning with salt and pepper, as needed.
6. Transfer the dip to a serving bowl and garnish with a few extra roasted baby artichokes and a sprinkle of Parmesan cheese.
7. Serve the dip with your favourite crackers, bread, or vegetables.

ROASTED CAULIFLOWER FLORETS DIP

Ingredients:
- 1 medium-sized head of cauliflower, cut into bite-sized florets
- 1 tablespoon olive oil
- 1 teaspoon garlic powder
- 1 teaspoon paprika
- Salt and pepper, to taste
- 1/2 cup Greek yogurt
- 2 tablespoons lemon juice
- 2 tablespoons chopped fresh parsley
- 1 tablespoon chopped fresh chives

Instructions:
1. Preheat the oven to 425 °F.
2. In a large mixing bowl, combine the cauliflower florets with the olive oil, garlic powder, paprika, salt, and pepper. Toss to coat evenly.
3. Spread the cauliflower florets in a single layer on a baking sheet lined with parchment paper.
4. Roast the cauliflower in the preheated oven for 20–25 minutes, until tender and lightly browned.
5. In a separate bowl, mix the Greek yogurt, lemon juice, parsley, and chives until well combined.
6. Once the cauliflower is done, transfer it to a serving dish and let it cool for a few minutes.
7. Spoon the yogurt mixture over the roasted cauliflower and use a spatula to gently mix everything together.
8. Serve the dip immediately, garnished with extra parsley and chives, if desired.

ROASTED RED PEPPER DIP

Ingredients:
- 1 can of roasted red peppers, drained and chopped
- 1/2 cup of Greek Yogurt
- 1/2 cup of regular, light or lactose-free cream cheese, softened
- 1/4 cup of grated Parmesan cheese
- 1 clove of garlic, minced
- 1 tablespoon of lemon juice
- 1/4 teaspoon of salt
- 1/4 teaspoon of black pepper
- 1 tablespoon of chopped fresh parsley (optional)

Instructions:
1. Start by draining and chopping the roasted red peppers from the can.
2. In a food processor or blender, combine the chopped red peppers, Greek Yogurt, cream cheese, Parmesan cheese, minced garlic, lemon juice, salt, and black pepper.
3. Pulse the mixture until it is smooth and well-combined.
4. If desired, add in the chopped fresh parsley and pulse again briefly to incorporate.
5. Transfer the dip to a serving bowl and cover it with plastic wrap.
6. Refrigerate the dip for at least an hour to allow the flavours to meld together.
7. Serve the roasted red pepper dip with your favourite crackers, chips, or vegetables.

OLD FAVOURITE ONION DIP

Ingredients:
- 2 cup Greek Yogurt
- 1 packet dried onion soup mix
- 1/4 teaspoon garlic powder
- 1/4 teaspoon onion powder
- 1/4 teaspoon dried dill weed
- Salt and pepper to taste

Instructions:
1. In a mixing bowl, Greek Yogurt
2. Add in the dried onion soup mix, garlic powder, onion powder, and dried dill weed. Mix until fully incorporated.
3. Taste the dip and add salt and pepper as desired.
4. Cover and refrigerate for at least 30 minutes to allow the flavours to meld together.
5. Serve with your favourite chips, crackers, or vegetables.

CREAMY COCONUT DIP

Ingredients:
- 1 cup coconut yogurt
- 1/4 cup finely chopped fresh coriander
- 2 tablespoons finely chopped red onion
- 2 cloves garlic, minced
- 1 teaspoon ground cumin
- 1/2 teaspoon salt
- Juice of 1/2 lime

Instructions:
1. In a medium bowl, whisk together the coconut yogurt, coriander, red onion, garlic, cumin, salt, and lime juice.
2. Taste the dip and adjust the seasoning as needed. You can add more salt, lime juice, or coriander depending on your preference.
3. Cover the bowl with plastic wrap and refrigerate the dip for at least 1 hour to allow the flavours to meld together.
4. Before serving, give the dip a good stir and transfer it to a serving bowl.
5. Serve the coconut yogurt dip with your favourite vegetables or chips for dipping. This dip pairs well with fresh cucumber slices, carrot sticks, or Pico sticks.

CREAMY CASHEW DIP

Ingredients:
- 1 cup raw cashews, soaked in water for at least 2 hours
- 1/4 cup water
- 2 tablespoons fresh lemon juice
- 2 cloves garlic, minced
- 1/2 teaspoon salt
- 1/4 teaspoon black pepper
- 1/4 teaspoon cumin
- 2 tablespoons chopped fresh parsley

Instructions:
1. Drain the soaked cashews and rinse them under cold water.
2. In a blender or food processor, combine the cashews, water, lemon juice, garlic, salt, black pepper, and cumin. Blend until smooth and creamy.
3. Transfer the dip to a bowl and stir in the chopped parsley.
4. Chill the dip in the refrigerator for at least 30 minutes before serving.
5. Serve with your favourite vegetables, crackers, or Pico sticks.

SUN-DRIED TOMATO N BEAN DIP

Ingredients:
- 1 jar (570g) white beans, drained and rinsed
- 1/2 cup jar sun-dried tomatoes, drained and roughly chopped
- 1/4 cup olive oil
- 1 or 2 cloves garlic, minced
- 1 tablespoon lemon juice
- 1/2 teaspoon salt
- 1/4 teaspoon black pepper
- 2 tablespoons chopped fresh parsley

Instructions:
1. In a food processor or blender, combine the white beans, sun-dried tomatoes, olive oil, garlic, lemon juice, salt, and pepper.
2. Pulse the mixture until it is smooth and creamy.
3. Transfer the dip to a serving bowl and sprinkle with fresh parsley.
4. Serve with Pico sticks, crackers, or sliced vegetables for dipping.

SIMPLE CHICKPEA DIP

Ingredients:
- 1 jar chickpeas, drained and rinsed
- 1/4 cup olive oil
- Juice of 1 lemon
- 2 cloves garlic, minced
- Salt and pepper, to taste
- Water (as needed to adjust consistency)
- Optional toppings: chopped parsley, paprika

Instructions:
1. In a food processor, pulse the chickpeas, olive oil, lemon juice, and garlic until well combined.
2. Add salt and pepper to taste.
3. If the dip is too thick, gradually add water and pulse until the desired consistency is reached.
4. Transfer the dip to a bowl and top with chopped parsley and red pepper flakes (if desired).
5. Serve with Pico sticks, veggies, or your favourite dipping accompaniment.

SPICED BEAN DIP

Ingredients:
- 1 jar of red beans, drained and rinsed
- 2 garlic cloves, minced
- 2 tablespoons of lemon juice
- 2 tablespoons of olive oil
- 1/2 teaspoon of ground cumin
- 1/2 teaspoon of sweet or hot paprika
- Salt and pepper to taste
- Chopped fresh parsley for garnish (optional)

Instructions:
1. In a food processor or blender, combine the red beans, minced garlic, lemon juice, olive oil, ground cumin, sweet or hot paprika, salt, and pepper.
2. Process until the mixture is smooth and creamy. If the mixture is too thick, you can add a tablespoon or two of water to thin it out.
3. Taste and adjust the seasoning as needed.
4. Transfer the dip to a serving bowl and garnish with chopped parsley, if desired.
5. Serve the dip with Pico sticks, tortilla chips, or cut-up vegetables like carrots, celery, and bell peppers.

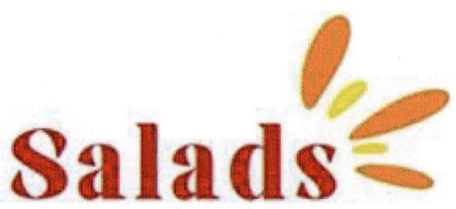

Salads

Salads are the first choice for many people when it comes to eating healthy, even on holiday.

Not only are they quick and easy to prepare, but they are also a practical option for those who want to maintain their healthy eating habits while on holiday.

Whether you are lounging on the beach or exploring a new city, a delicious salad provides the perfect balance of nutrients and flavours to keep you feeling full and energised throughout the day.

Plus, salads are a great way to incorporate a variety of fresh fruits, vegetables and lean protein into your diet, making them a healthy option for anyone looking to eat a balanced diet.

Whether you want to stay fit and healthy or just need a quick and easy meal on the go, salads are a convenient and delicious choice for any holiday or even if you are just staying at home.

SOUTH SEAS SALAD

Ingredients:
- 2 cups mixed greens
- 1/2 cup sliced cucumber
- 1/2 cup sliced red onion
- 1/2 cup cherry tomatoes
- 1/4 cup chopped fresh coriander
- 1/4 cup peanut powder
- 2 tablespoons lime juice
- 1 tablespoon honey
- 1 tablespoon soy sauce
- 1 tablespoon olive oil
- ¼ cup sesame seeds
- Salt and pepper to taste

Instructions:
1. In a large bowl, combine the mixed greens, cucumber, red onion, cherry tomatoes, and coriander.
2. In a separate small bowl, whisk together the peanut powder, lime juice, honey, soy sauce, sesame oil, and a pinch of salt and pepper until well combined.
3. Pour the peanut dressing over the salad and toss well to coat.
4. Serve immediately and enjoy your delicious and nutritious salad with a hint of peanut flavour!

SOUTH SEAS CHICKPEA SALAD

Ingredients:
- 1 jar of chickpeas, drained and rinsed
- 2 cups of mixed salad greens
- 1/2 cup of sliced cucumber
- 1/2 cup of sliced bell pepper
- 1/4 cup of chopped red onion
- 1/4 cup of chopped fresh parsley
- 2 tablespoons of peanut powder
- 2 tablespoons of olive oil
- 1 tablespoon of apple cider vinegar
- 1 tablespoon of honey
- Salt and black pepper, to taste

Instructions:
1. In a large mixing bowl, combine the chickpeas, salad greens, cucumber, bell pepper, red onion, and parsley.
2. In a separate small mixing bowl, whisk together the peanut powder, olive oil, apple cider vinegar, honey, salt, and black pepper until well combined.
3. Pour the peanut dressing over the salad and toss until all the ingredients are evenly coated.
4. Serve immediately and enjoy your delicious and healthy peanut powder and chickpea salad!

RED BEAN N AVOCADO SALAD

Ingredients:
- 1 jar of red beans, drained and rinsed
- 1 red bell pepper, diced
- 1 small red onion, diced
- 1 cup cherry tomatoes, halved
- 1/2 cup fresh coriander, chopped
- 1 avocado, diced
- 1 lime, juiced
- 2 tablespoons olive oil
- Salt and pepper to taste

Instructions:
1. In a large mixing bowl, combine the drained and rinsed red beans, diced red bell pepper, diced red onion, halved cherry tomatoes, and chopped coriander.
2. In a small bowl, whisk together the lime juice, olive oil, salt, and pepper.
3. Pour the dressing over the salad and toss until all ingredients are well coated.
4. Add the diced avocado and gently mix in.
5. Chill the salad in the fridge for at least 30 minutes before serving.

WHITE BEAN N FRESH SALAD

Ingredients:
- 1 jar of white beans, drained and rinsed
- 1/2 red onion, finely chopped
- 1/2 red bell pepper, diced
- 1/4 cup chopped fresh parsley
- 1/4 cup chopped fresh coriander
- 2 tablespoons olive oil
- 1 tablespoon apple cider vinegar
- 1 teaspoon honey
- Salt and pepper to taste

Instructions:
1. In a large bowl, combine the white beans, chopped red onion, diced red bell pepper, fresh parsley, and coriander.
2. In a separate small bowl, whisk together the olive oil, apple cider vinegar, honey, salt, and pepper until well combined.
3. Pour the dressing over the salad ingredients and toss until everything is evenly coated.
4. Serve immediately or chill in the refrigerator until ready to serve.

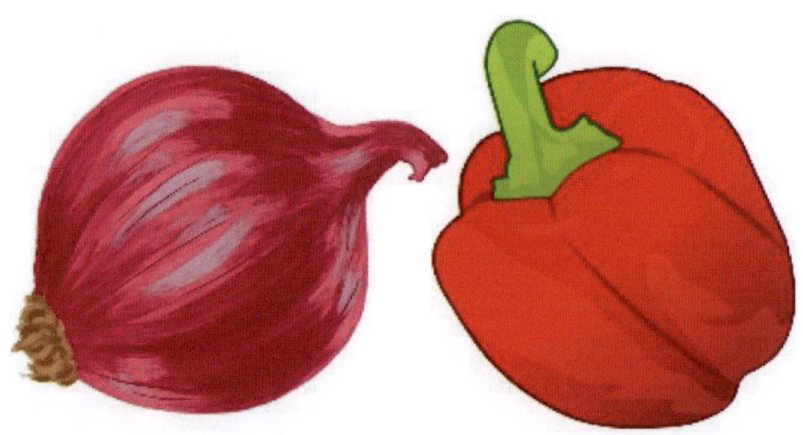

FRESH BURGOS LACTOSE-FREE CHEESE SALAD

Ingredients:
- 4 cups mixed greens
- 1/2 cup cherry tomatoes, halved
- 1/2 cup cucumber, sliced
- 1/4 cup red onion, sliced
- 1/4 cup fresh basil leaves, chopped
- 1/4 cup fresh mint leaves, chopped
- 1/4 cup fresh parsley leaves, chopped
- 1/4 cup (1 unit 62 gr.) chopped lactose-free fresh Burgos cheese
- 2 tablespoons extra-virgin olive oil
- 1 tablespoon balsamic vinegar
- Salt and pepper to taste

Instructions:
1. In a large bowl, combine the mixed greens, cherry tomatoes, cucumber, and red onion.
2. In a separate bowl, whisk together the olive oil, balsamic vinegar, salt, and pepper.
3. Pour the dressing over the salad and toss to combine.
4. Sprinkle the fresh basil, mint, and parsley over the top of the salad.
5. Toss the lactose-free fresh cheese over the top of the salad.

SPANISH CAPRESE SALAD

Ingredients:
- 3 large ripe tomatoes
- 8 ounces fresh mozzarella cheese.Light or normal
- 1/4 cup fresh basil leaves
- 2 tablespoons extra-virgin olive oil
- 2 teaspoons balsamic vinegar
- Salt and pepper to taste

Instructions:
1. Slice the tomatoes and arrange them on a serving platter.
2. Top the tomatoes with slices of fresh mozzarella cheese.
3. Tear the basil leaves into small pieces and sprinkle them over the cheese and tomatoes.
4. Drizzle the olive oil and balsamic vinegar over the salad.
5. Sprinkle with salt and pepper to taste.

FRESH SUMMER SALAD WITH SOYA BITES

Ingredients:
- 1 cup textured soya
- 2 cups mixed greens (spinach, lettuce, arugula, etc.)
- 1/2 cup cherry tomatoes, halved
- 1/2 cup cucumber, sliced
- 1/4 cup red onion, sliced
- 1/4 cup fresh parsley, chopped
- 1/2 cup feta cheese cube
- 2 tablespoons olive oil
- 1 tablespoon lemon juice
- 1 garlic clove, minced
- 1 teaspoon Dijon mustard
- Salt and pepper, to taste

Instructions:
1. Begin by rehydrating the textured soya according to package instructions, 1 to 1 .
2. Once the textured soya is rehydrated, drain any excess water and set it aside.
3. In a large bowl, combine the mixed greens, cherry tomatoes, cucumber, red onion, parsley, and crumbled feta cheese.
4. In a separate small bowl, whisk together the olive oil, lemon juice, minced garlic, Dijon mustard, salt, and pepper to make the dressing.
5. Add the rehydrated textured soya to the salad and toss to combine.
6. Drizzle the dressing over the salad and toss again to evenly coat.
7. Serve immediately and enjoy!

PEANUT LOVERS SOYA SALAD

Ingredients:
- 1 cup textured soya
- 1/2 cup peanut powder
- 1/2 cup chopped tomatoes
- 1/2 cup chopped cucumber
- 1/2 cup chopped onions
- 1/4 cup chopped coriander
- 2 cloves garlic, minced
- 2 tablespoons olive oil
- 1 tablespoon lemon juice
- Salt and pepper, to taste

Instructions:
1. Begin by rehydrating the textured soya according to package instructions. Normally, 1 mix to 1 water. Drain any excess water and set aside.
2. In a small bowl, mix together the peanut powder and minced garlic until well combined.
3. In a separate bowl, combine the chopped tomatoes, cucumber, onions, and coriander.
4. Add the rehydrated textured soya to the bowl of vegetables and mix well.
5. Drizzle the olive oil and lemon juice over the salad and toss to coat.
6. Sprinkle the peanut powder and garlic mixture over the salad and mix well.
7. Season with salt and pepper to taste.
8. Serve immediately and enjoy!

MEXICAN CORN SALAD

Ingredients:
- 2 cup of frozen sweet corn (thawed / rinsed)
- 2 cups of cherry tomatoes, halved
- 1/2 red onion, thinly sliced
- 1/2 cup of fresh coriander, chopped
- 1 jalapeño pepper, seeded and finely chopped
- 2 tablespoons of lime juice
- 2 tablespoons of olive oil
- Salt and pepper to taste

Instructions:
1. In a large bowl, combine the sweet corn, cherry tomatoes, red onion, coriander, and jalapeño pepper.
2. In a separate small bowl, whisk together the lime juice, olive oil, salt, and pepper.
3. Pour the dressing over the corn and tomato mixture and toss to combine.
4. Serve chilled as a side dish or a light meal.

ROASTED RED PEPPER N PINE NUT SALAD

Ingredients:
- 1 can of roasted red peppers, drained and chopped
- 2 cups of mixed salad greens
- 1/4 cup of sliced red onions
- 1/4 cup of crumbled feta cheese
- 1/4 cup of toasted pine nuts
- 2 tablespoons of balsamic vinegar
- 2 tablespoons of olive oil
- Salt and pepper to taste

Instructions:
1. In a large mixing bowl, combine the mixed salad greens and chopped roasted red peppers.
2. Add the sliced red onions, crumbled feta cheese. Mix everything together.
3. In a frying pan, toast the pine nuts till light brown.
4. In a small mixing bowl, whisk together the balsamic vinegar and olive oil. Season with salt and pepper to taste.
5. Drizzle the dressing over the salad mixture in the large mixing bowl. Toss everything together until the salad is evenly coated with the dressing. Top with pine nuts.

WALNUT N CRANBERRY SALAD

Ingredients:
- 1 head of romaine lettuce
- 1/2 cup of natural walnuts, chopped
- 1/4 cup of crumbled feta cheese
- 1/4 red onion, sliced
- 1/4 cup of dried cranberries
- 1/4 cup of balsamic vinaigrette
- Salt and pepper to taste

Instructions:
1. Wash and chop the romaine lettuce into bite-sized pieces.
2. In a small pan, toast the chopped walnuts over medium heat until they become fragrant and slightly browned. Set aside.
3. Add the sliced red onion, crumbled feta cheese, and dried cranberries to the romaine lettuce.
4. Pour the balsamic vinaigrette over the top of the salad, and toss well to coat.
5. Sprinkle the toasted walnuts over the top of the salad, and add salt and pepper to taste.

QUINOA SUMMER SALAD

Ingredients:
- 1 cup quinoa, rinsed and drained
- 2 cups water
- 1/4 cup olive oil
- 1/4 cup freshly squeezed lemon juice
- 2 cloves garlic, minced
- 1 teaspoon honey
- Salt and freshly ground black pepper, to taste
- 1 red bell pepper, diced
- 1 yellow bell pepper, diced
- 1 cucumber, diced
- 1/2 cup chopped fresh parsley
- 1/2 cup cubed feta cheese
- 1/4 cup chopped walnuts

Instructions:
1. In a medium saucepan, combine quinoa and water. Bring to a boil, then reduce heat to low and simmer for about 15–20 minutes, or until the water is absorbed, and the quinoa is tender. Remove from heat and let cool.
2. In a small bowl, whisk together olive oil, lemon juice, garlic, honey, salt, and pepper to make the dressing.
3. In a large bowl, combine the cooked quinoa, diced bell peppers, diced cucumber, chopped parsley, crumbled feta cheese, and chopped walnuts.
4. Pour the dressing over the salad and toss gently to combine.
5. Serve immediately or refrigerate until ready to serve. Enjoy!

ASIAN QUINOA SALAD

Ingredients:
- 1 cup cooked quinoa
- 2 cups mixed salad greens
- 1/2 cup diced cucumber
- 1/2 cup cherry tomatoes, halved
- 1/4 cup sliced red onion
- 1/4 cup chopped fresh coriander
- 1/4 cup chopped roasted peanuts
- 2 tablespoons peanut powder
- 2 tablespoons olive oil
- 1 tablespoon apple cider vinegar
- 1 tablespoon honey
- Salt and pepper to taste

Instructions:
1. In a large bowl, combine the cooked quinoa, mixed salad greens, diced cucumber, cherry tomatoes, red onion, and coriander.
2. In a separate bowl, whisk together the peanut powder, olive oil, apple cider vinegar, honey, salt, and pepper until well combined.
3. Pour the dressing over the salad and toss until everything is well coated.
4. Sprinkle chopped roasted peanuts on top of the salad just before serving.
5. Serve chilled and enjoy!

CHICKPEA N BABY SPINACH SALAD

Ingredients:
- 1 jar of chickpeas, drained and rinsed
- 1/2 cup sun-dried tomatoes, drained and roughly chopped
- 1/2 red onion, thinly sliced
- 2 cups baby spinach leaves
- 1/4 cup crumbled feta cheese
- 1/4 cup chopped fresh parsley
- 1/4 cup extra-virgin olive oil
- 2 tablespoons red wine vinegar
- Salt and black pepper to taste

Instructions:
1. In a large mixing bowl, combine the chickpeas, sun-dried tomatoes, red onion, baby spinach leaves, feta cheese, and parsley.
2. In a small bowl, whisk together the olive oil, red wine vinegar, salt, and black pepper to make the dressing.
3. Pour the dressing over the salad and toss until all the ingredients are evenly coated.
4. Divide the salad into individual bowls or plates and serve immediately.

CHICKEN N GREEN OLIVE SALAD

Ingredients:
- 1/2 pound cooked chicken breast, sliced or shredded
- 1/2 cup sliced green olives without pits
- 1/2 cup sliced cherry tomatoes
- 1/2 cup sliced cucumber
- 1/4 cup chopped red onion
- 1/4 cup chopped fresh parsley
- 2 tablespoons extra-virgin olive oil
- 1 tablespoon red wine vinegar
- Salt and freshly ground black pepper to taste

Instructions:
1. In a large mixing bowl, combine the cooked chicken, green olives, cherry tomatoes, cucumber, red onion, and parsley.
2. In a small bowl, whisk together the olive oil, red wine vinegar, salt, and pepper until well combined.
3. Pour the dressing over the salad ingredients and toss well to coat.
4. Serve the salad immediately or refrigerate until ready to serve.

CHICKEN N ALMOND SALAD

Ingredients:
- 2 chicken breasts, cooked and diced
- 1 head of romaine lettuce, washed and chopped
- 1/2 cup cherry tomatoes, halved
- 1/2 red onion, sliced
- 1/2 cup chopped almonds
- 1 avocado, diced
- 1/4 cup olive oil
- 2 tablespoons lemon juice
- 1 tablespoon Dijon mustard
- Salt and pepper to taste

Instructions:
1. Cook the chicken breasts in a pan or on a grill until fully cooked. Dice the chicken into small pieces and set aside.
2. Wash and chop the romaine lettuce and place it in a large mixing bowl.
3. Add the halved cherry tomatoes, sliced red onion, sliced almonds, and diced avocado to the bowl with the romaine lettuce.
4. In a small mixing bowl, whisk together the olive oil, lemon juice, Dijon mustard, salt, and pepper.
5. Pour the dressing over the salad mixture and toss to combine.
6. Add the cooked diced chicken to the salad and toss gently.
7. Serve immediately and enjoy your delicious romaine lettuce and chicken salad!

MIXED GREENS N BLACK OLIVE SALAD

Ingredients:
- 4 cups mixed greens (e.g., lettuce, arugula, spinach)
- 1/2 red onion, sliced thinly
- 1/2 cucumber, sliced
- 1/2 red bell pepper, diced
- 1/2 cup black olives without pits, sliced
- 1/4 cup extra-virgin olive oil
- 2 tablespoons red wine vinegar
- 1 teaspoon Dijon mustard
- Salt and black pepper, to taste

Instructions:
1. Begin by washing and drying the mixed greens and adding them to a large salad bowl.
2. Add the sliced red onion, cucumber, and diced red bell pepper to the salad bowl.
3. Slice the black olives without pits and add them to the salad.
4. In a small bowl, whisk together the extra-virgin olive oil, red wine vinegar, and Dijon mustard until the mixture is emulsified.
5. Drizzle the dressing over the salad and toss to combine.
6. Season the salad with salt and black pepper, to taste.

LENTIL FUSILLI PASTA SALAD

Ingredients:
- 8 oz fusilli pasta made with lentils
- 1 red bell pepper, diced
- 1 yellow bell pepper, diced
- 1 small red onion, diced
- 1 cup cherry tomatoes, halved
- 1/2 cup black olives, pitted and sliced
- 1/4 cup chopped fresh parsley
- 1/4 cup chopped fresh basil
- 1/4 cup extra-virgin olive oil
- 2 tablespoons red wine vinegar
- Salt and freshly ground black pepper to taste

Instructions:
1. Cook the Fusilli pasta in salted water according to the package instructions until it is al dente. Drain and rinse with cold water.
2. In a large bowl, combine the cooked Fusilli pasta, diced red and yellow bell peppers, diced red onion, halved cherry tomatoes, sliced black olives, chopped fresh parsley, and chopped fresh basil.
3. In a small bowl, whisk together the extra-virgin olive oil and red wine vinegar. Pour the dressing over the salad and toss until everything is coated evenly.
4. Season with salt and freshly ground black pepper to taste.
5. Chill the salad in the refrigerator for at least 30 minutes before serving.

PARDINA LENTIL SALAD

Ingredients:
- 1 can of pardina lentils, drained and rinsed
- 2 cups of arugula or mixed greens
- 1/2 red onion, sliced
- 1/2 cup of cherry tomatoes, halved
- 1 avocado, diced
- 1/4 cup of chopped fresh parsley
- 1/4 cup of chopped fresh coriander
- 1/4 cup of lemon juice
- 1/4 cup of olive oil
- Salt and pepper to taste

Instructions:
1. In a large mixing bowl, combine the lentils, arugula or mixed greens, sliced red onion, cherry tomatoes, avocado, parsley, and coriander.
2. In a small mixing bowl, whisk together the lemon juice, olive oil, salt, and pepper to make the dressing.
3. Pour the dressing over the salad and toss to combine.
4. Divide the salad into individual serving bowls and enjoy!

TRANSLATED GLOSSARY
INGREDIENTS & SPICES

Cheese - queso
Cream cheese - queso crema
Parmesan cheese - queso parmesano
Lactose-free fresh cheese - queso fresco sin lactosa
Mozzarella cheese - queso mozzarella
Feta cheese - queso feta
Yogurt - yogur
Mayonnaise - mayonesa
Honey - Miel
Jalapeño peppers - chiles jalapeños
Soy sauce - salsa de soja
Sesame oil - aceite de sésamo
Apple cider vinegar - vinagre de sidra de manzana
Balsamic vinegar - vinagre balsámico
Lime juice - jugo de limón
Lemon juice - jugo de limon
Olive oil - aceite de oliva
Dijon mustard - mostaza de Dijon
Sun-dried tomatoes - tomates secados al sol

Tomatoes - tomates
Onions - cebollas
Garlic - ajo
Avocado - aguacate
Roasted red peppers - pimientos rojos asados
Artichoke hearts - corazones de alcachofa
Baby artichokes - pequeñas alcachofas
Cauliflower florets - floretes de coliflor
Spinach - espinacas
Chives - cebollín
Cucumber - pepino
Lettuce - lechuga
Arugula - rúcula
Romaine lettuce - lechuga romana

Dried cranberries - arándanos secos
Pine nuts - piñones
Cashews - anacardos
Almonds - almendras
Peanuts - cacahuates
Walnuts - nueces

Sweet Paprika - Pimentón Dulce
Hot Paprika - Pimentón Picante
Coriander - cilantro
Salt - Sal
Pepper - Pimienta
Garlic powder - Ajo en polvo
Onion powder - Cebolla en polvo
Cumin - Comino
Turmeric - Cúrcuma
Parsley - Perejil
Basil - Albahaca
Dill - eneldo
Mint leaves - hojas de menta
Coriander - cilantro

Printed by Amazon Italia Logistica S.r.l.
Torrazza Piemonte (TO), Italy